Python Crash C

The Ultimate Step-By-Step Guide to Learn, Understand, and Master Python Programming and Computer Coding Language (From Beginners to Advanced)

By James Deep

derived from various sources. Please consult a licensed professional before attempting any techniques outlined in this book.

By reading this document, the reader agrees that under no circumstances is the author responsible for any losses, direct or indirect, which are incurred as a result of the use of information contained within this document, including, but not limited to, — errors, omissions, or inaccuracies.

Table of Contents

Introduction... 1

Chapter 1: What is the Python Language? 3

The Benefits of Python 7

It is Easy to Work with 7

It Has Lots of Power 8

Many Libraries to Work With 9

Easy to Read 9

It is an OOP Language.................................... 10

The Basics of the Python Language 10

Python Keywords... 11

Naming Our Identifiers 11

Control Flow Basics 12

Python Comments 13

Variables 14

Operators 15

Chapter 2: Everything You Need to Know to Install Python 16

Installing On the Mac Operating System 17

The Windows Operating System.................................. 19

The Linux System.. 23

Chapter 3: The Python Variables and Strings........ 26

The Python Variables 27

The Python Strings *30*

Chapter 4: Handling Python Operators, Tuples, and Lists **34**

The Python Operators *35*

Arithmetic Operators 35

Comparison Operators 36

Logical Operators 37

Assignment Operators 38

Understanding Tuples and Lists *39*

The Lists 40

The Tuples 41

Chapter 5: The Python Functions **43**

.... *44*

Why are User Defined Functions So Important? *45*

Options for Function Arguments *46*

Writing a Function *48*

Chapter 6: Python as an OOP Language and Working with the Python Classes **50**

How to Write a Class *53*

Working with the Access Class *55*

Chapter 7: The Conditional Statements in Python . **58**

The If Conditional Statements *59*

The If Else Conditional Statement 61

The Elif Conditional Statement 64

Chapter 8: The Python Loops **68**

.... **68**

The While Loop 71

Working with the For Loop 73

The Nested Loop 75

Chapter 9: Handling Your Own Exceptions **78**

.... **78**

How to Raise An Exception 80

How to Define My Own Exceptions 84

Chapter 10: Python Encapsulation **87**

.... **87**

The Getter and Setter 89

Putting It All Together 90

What to Keep In Mind 94

Chapter 11: Python Databases & Dictionaries and How to Work with Them **96**

.... **96**

The Python Database 97

The Python Dictionaries 101

Chapter 12: Working with GUI and CGI in This Language **110**

.... **110**

Getting Familiar with GUI *110*

What is CGI? *113*

Conclusion **118**

Introduction

The following chapters will discuss all of the different parts of learning how to do some of your coding in the Python language. There are a lot of different reasons why you will want to learn how to work with the Python language, and we want to make sure that we can take some of the steps of the different part by step and learn how to make them work for our needs. There are a lot of options out there for learning how to code and get things done with programming, but you will find that the Python language is going to be one of the best ones to work with. And this guidebook will show you why that is.

This guidebook is going to spend some time taking a look at some of the basics of the Python language. We will look at what Python is all about, where it comes from, and even the steps that are needed to install this language and all of the necessary files on your computer, no matter what operating system you are working with at the time.

Once we have some of the basics of coding in the Python language down, it is time for us to move on to the next step. In this one, we are going to explore a few other important parts that come with Python including how to handle things like the variables and the strings, how to work with lists, tuples, and operators, and some of the Python functions to get things done. All of these are important to writing out some of the various codes that you want to handle in the Python language, and should not be missed out on.

Once we have some of the basic parts of the Python language down and ready to go, it is time for us to work on some of the actual codes that we need to write to gain some expertise in this kind of language. We will look a bit at how to write out own classes while gaining a deeper understanding of the OOP aspect of Python, how to write out conditional statements loops, and even some exceptions of your own.

To finish off some of the topics that we need to know to get started with programming in Python, there are a few more things that a beginner should understand to get the best results. We will spend our time in these chapters with a look at Python encapsulation and what this means for keeping certain parts of your code private and secrete, what the databases and dictionaries mean in this language, and how to work with CGI and GUI in this language as well.

There are so many great things that we are going to take a look at when it is time to work with the Python language. This guidebook is going to spend some time taking a look at some of the most important parts that come with this kind of language, and how even a beginner can get started and make this language their own. When you are ready to learn a bit more about this language and what it can do for you, make sure to check out this guidebook to help out!

Chapter 1: What is the Python Language?

History and Evolution

Since computers were first invented, many people have had the job to make them more useful. To make this happen, there are a ton of programming tools that have been developed over the years to turn the instructions the computer is given into code that the computer can execute. When this first started, assembly language was the main type. While it did allow you to create programming that was tailored and then optimized for the low memory systems of that time, it was hard to learn, read, and maintain and only a few people could use it.

As computer technology grew and many systems became more complex, the programming languages needed to change as well. Some higher-level languages including Lisp, Cobol, and Fortran were produced to produce punch cards which the computers were able to read and then execute the instructions that were found on the card. Programming with this kind of tool was a lot easier than the languages in the past, allowing more people to write the complex programs they needed.

As time started to go on, there were a lot of improvements that were made to some of the technology that we are working with now, and it has resulted in a lot of better storage methods when it comes to our programs and more. For example, some of those punch cards have been replaced with a type of magnetic tape and then it was all moved over to work with a disc drive. As these new inventions came out, the tools to work on these programs improved as well.

Basic was one of the first coding languages that was designed to be easy to read through and this one was developed in the 1960s. then in the 1970s, we saw the introduction of Pascal and C, and these became tools that helped us to get a really simple and structured kind of programming language that would help a programmer to get the efficient code that they want. You will find that the structured languages like these would not have to rely on the go-to statement found in some of the other languages. Instead, these programs would rely on a flow that has features including conditional statements, functions, and loops like we will talk about later in this guidebook. These features were nice because they would allow a new programmer to make their own applications with the help of standalone reusable routines, which would then be able to lower the amount of time that it would take to develop the program, and even debug it so that the program would work the way that you would like.

It was in the 1980's when the next big advancement in programming happened This was where C++, and a few other languages, turned into OOP languages, or object-oriented programming languages. There are a number of these that are now available and usable, but they were useful because they helped us to hold onto our information better. While these tools of OOP languages were powerful and had some new capabilities when it came to coding, many times they would be seen as special because they could cut out some of the challenges that came with coding.

As the use and the popularity of computers started to grow, and it becomes common for more people to use them, it was also an important factor to have a language for programming that was easy to use, one that we can use on a lot of different platforms. Because of this need, the language that we know as Python today was developed.

Python is going to be a general-purpose programming language. Whether you are a beginner or someone who has been in the coding world for some time, you will find that this language is easy to learn while still making sure that there is a lot of power behind it to get those codes done. You are able to use this for a lot of different purposes, from some general housekeeping tasks for your system to just having fun and making your programs and games.

Of course, when you compare this language to some of the others out there, you will also notice that Python is going to have a lot of rules and structures that you must follow to get this to work. No matter what codes you would like to write in Python, you will need to follow the rules and ensure that the compiler is ready to handle it all. The good news is that the rules are pretty simple with this language and you will find that this language is simple, powerful, and compact all in one. As a beginner, it is easier to catch onto this kind of coding language than you think, and before long, and with the help of this guidebook, you will be able to get everything to work the way you would like and will be writing your codes in no time.

In the past, a lot of people were worried about learning a coding language. They worried that these languages were too tough to learn, that they would just get frustrated, and that only those who had spent their whole lives around computers could even attempt to write their codes. And maybe with some of the older codes, this was true. Thanks to a lot of the newer codes that have been introduced recently, the idea that only those gifted in computer programming could code has faded away. With many of the codes that are coming out now, including Python, anyone can learn a few of the syntaxes for what they want to do, or even find some premade codes online and make some changes. And since many of these codes are open-sourced, it is easier than ever to learn how to use them and develop the codes to meet your needs.

You will find that many of the modern languages that are used for coding are going to be a lot better and easier to use than what we were able to find in the past with most coding languages. Gone are the days that even professionals would run into troubles regularly when it was time to find the bugs in the system. Now it is possible for anyone and everyone to learn how to use this coding language for these needs. And this is mainly because we have a lot of great OOP languages to work within Python.

The Benefits of Python

There are a lot of benefits that come with using the Python coding language for all of your programming needs. It is often seen as one of the best general-purpose coding languages that you can work with, and with the ease of use and learning, and all of the great features that come with it, it is no wonder that this language is a favorite for a lot of people along the way.

It is Easy to Work with

The first benefit that most people are going to enjoy when it comes to using the Python language is that it is very easy to use. This language was designed for use with a beginner, and the whole purpose is to make sure that anyone, even those who may not be well-versed in doing any kind of programming at all, will be able to learn and write some of the codes of their own that they would like. This language is meant to help a beginner, someone who has never had a chance to work with coding in the past, learn how to do some of this coding, and get the results that they would like. There are also a lot of different things that you are able to do when you work with the Python coding language. It is designed to help with almost any kind of coding that you are interested in handling, from some of the basics of writing your own projects all the way to helping out with data analysis and machine learning if you so choose. There is just so much that you are able to do with this kind of language and many people are jumping on board to learn how to work all of these different angles with ease thanks to the Python coding language.

It Has Lots of Power

Even though this is a coding language that is meant to help us out with some of the basics of coding, you will find that there is quite a bit of strength and power behind what we can do with it. Even more advanced problems can be easily handled when we are looking at this kind of language, and you will find that with the added extensions and libraries that are available with Python, it is easy to figure out how to write codes that work with some complex coding and programming problems

Some people hear about how easy it is to work with Python and they worry that there is not going to be enough strength and power behind it in order to get started. They think they need to go with another option because this one will not have the strength of the features that are needed to get things done. But, once you mess around with some of the codes that we will do with this language, you will find that it is going to have plenty of the power and a ton of the features, that you need to get anything done.

Many Libraries to Work With

While we are at it, you will find that a lot of the libraries and extensions that come with the Python language are going to be really great as well. You can already do a lot of work with the standard Python language, but you will also find that there are additional libraries that work well with Python and can help us to expand out what we are able to do with programming in this language. From libraries that can help us out with math, science, machine learning, data science, and more, you will find that the Python coding language is one of the best options for you to work with. From here, we will also find that the Python language is going to be one that is able to work well with others. For some of the basics that we will discuss in this guidebook, this is not going to seem like that big of a deal. But when we get into some things like machine learning and data science with this language, the fact that we can combine Python with other languages is going to help us get more done.

Easy to Read

We will also see that the Python coding language is going to be a great option to work with when you want to make sure that things stay organized and easy to read through. There are a lot of other coding languages out there that you can choose from, but that does not mean that they are the right ones for you. In most cases, beginners are going to find that working with an OOP language, just like Python is, is one of the best ways to keep the information organized and easy to use.

It is an OOP Language

The fact that Python is an OOP language is going to be good news for you. We will explore this a bit more in the next few chapters, but this basically means that the code is split up into classes, and then the objects that show up in the code will fit into one of these classes. This is the best way to make the code as efficient as possible, and will ensure that you are able to bring up the right parts, at the right times so that your code will work the way that you want.

As we can see here, there are a lot of different benefits that come with working in the Python language, and how well you will be able to use it. Sure, there are a lot of other coding languages out there that you are able to choose to work with. But none are going to provide us with as many benefits and features as we are going to be able to see with the Python language.

The Basics of the Python Language

Now that we know a bit more about the Python language and some of the things that we are able to do in order to see results with this kind of language, it is time to learn a few of the different basic parts that are needed in this kind of coding language before you even write out a single code with it at all. There are a lot of different parts that come into play, so let's dive right in and get started.

Python Keywords

The first thing that we need to take a look at in this section is the Python keywords. Just like with other languages that we may work with, we will find that these are reserved words that we are able to use to provide a command to our compiler. You should make sure that they are only used in the proper place in your code and that you are not bringing them up randomly, or you will end up with an error in the code that you are writing. These are reserved because they are meant to provide your compiler with the instructions that it needs in order to handle your coding at that time. these keywords are already programmed into the compiler to make sure that it behaves well. Because of this, you will find that they are going to be important to any kind of code that you are trying to write. Make sure that you learn what these works are all about, and how they are going to work with the compiler, so that you can be on the lookout.

Naming Our Identifiers

Your identifiers can be important to your code as well, and in Python, there are quite a few identifiers to work with too. You will find that they come in at a lot of different names and you may seem them as functions, entities, variables, and classes. When you are naming an identifier, you can use the same information and the same rules will apply for each of them, which makes it easier for you to remember the rules.

The first rule to remember is when you name these identifiers. You have many options when you are naming your identifiers. For example, you can rely on both uppercase and lowercase letters with naming, as well as any number and the underscore symbol. You can also combine any of these together. One thing to remember here is that you can't start the name with a number and there shouldn't be any spaces between the words that you write out. So, you can't write out 3words as a name, but you can write out words3 or threewords. Make sure that you don't use one of the keywords that we discussed above or you will end up with an error.

When you pick out the identifier name, you can follow the rules above, and try to pick out a name that you can remember. Later on, when writing the code, you will need to pull it back up, and if you give it a name that is difficult to remember, you could run into problems or raise errors because things aren't showing up the way that you want. Outside of these rules, you will be fine naming the identifiers anything that you want.

Control Flow Basics

In many languages, the control flow that comes with it is going to be an important thing as well. The control flow that comes with Python is going to be pretty important as well because it helps us to know whether or not we are correctly writing the code. There are going to be a few strings that we need to pay careful attention to because they need to be read by the compiler properly.

If you are not using the control flow in the right manner, then you will end up with the compiler being confused and then you will get some error messages. The good news here is that we are going to spend some time looking at a lot of examples of codes in this guidebook, and you will be able to figure out what is right and what is wrong with the control flow that you are working with.

Python Comments

The next thing that we need to spend some time on is the comments. As you are working with some of the codes that you would like to write, you may find that there are some situations where you would like to add in a little note, or some other explanation on what is being written inside of that particular code. And you want to be able to do this without causing the compiler to get confused or making it impossible to finish up the code without an error.

These are little notes that can be important to others who are using or reading through the code, but we do not want them to show up in the code when it is executed. And this is going to be known as a comment in the Python language, as well as with some of the other coding languages that you want to work with. Any comment that you write out with Python will be ignored and passed over by the compiler, as long as you use the # symbol ahead of what you are writing. This symbol is going to tell the compiler that you are writing out a comment, and that it should avoid reading that comment and instead move on to another part of the code to handle.

With the Python language, you technically are able to add in as many of these comments as you would like to help explain to yourself or others what you have written at that part of the code. If you would like to have one on every other line of the code, then this is technically allowed. Keep in mind though that this is going to make your code look a bit messy and unprofessional, so it is generally something that is avoided. Just add in the number of comments that are needed and don't go overboard, and your code will work great.

We will talk about the next two topics a bit more in some of the following chapters because they are so important to what we are going to be doing throughout our coding experience, but they still deserve a bit of mention here. We are going to take some time to look at two more important topics that are the basis of your Python code, whether these codes are simple or more complex, including the operators and variables.

Variables

Variables are another part of the code that you will need to know about because they are so common in your code. The variables are there to help store some of the values that you place in the code, helping them to stay organized and nice. You can easily add in some of the values to the right variable simply by using the equal sign. It is even possible for you to take two values and add it to the same variables if you want and you will see this occur in a few of the codes that we discuss through this guidebook. Variables are very common and you will easily see them throughout the examples that we show.

Operators

Then we are able to move on to some of the operators that you will be able to use. While you are coding you will quickly notice that these operators are all over the place. And there are quite a few of them that you are able to handle along the way as well. Learning how to work with these operators can make code writing a little bit easier, and will help us to make sure that our codes will work the way that we want.

Operators are pretty simple parts of your code, but you should still know how they work. You will find that there are a few different types of them that work well. For example, the arithmetic functions are great for helping you to add, divide, subtract, and multiply different parts of the code together. There are assignment operators that will assign a specific value to your variable so that the compiler knows how to treat this. There are also comparison operators that will allow you to look at a few different pieces of code and then determine if they are similar or not and how the computer should react based on that information.

These are just a few of the different parts of working with the Python code that we are able to focus on. These parts are going to be critical to ensuring that we are not going to lose out on some of the work that we need to handle, and can make it easier for us to understand some of the more complex codes that we will focus on at a later time. Make sure to review these parts and gain a good understanding of how they work to help make it a bit easier when it is time to work with the codes that are coming up.

Chapter 2: Everything You Need to Know to Install Python

Before you are able to work with any of the coding that we want to do with Python or anything else that comes in this guidebook, we need to take a moment to learn more about how to install and download this language on your own computer. The good news is that the Python language can work on any operating system that you would like. You are not limited based on the system that you want to work with, which is another great benefit that you will be able to enjoy when it is time to work with this kind of language.

With this in mind, we want to make sure that we know all of the rules that need to be in place to install Python appropriately, no matter what kind of operating system you are working with. We are going to take a look at the three biggest systems out there that you can work with including Mac OS X, Windows, and the Linux operating system to help us get started.

Installing On the Mac Operating System

First on the list is the Mac OS X system. If you are working with a computer that has this on it, you may find that there is already a version of Python 2 on that system. Many of the Mac computers are going to come pre-installed with the Python library on them, which makes it easier to use them and get the results that you would like overall. The version you have though is going to depend on which type of computer you have and how long you have owned it. To check out which version of Python 2 is on your system, you can type in the following prompt in your command terminal:

Python – V

This is going to show you the version you get so a number will come up. You can also choose to install Python 3 on this system if you would like, and it isn't required to uninstall the 2.X version on the computer. To check for the 3.X installation, you just need to open up the terminal app and then type in the following prompt:

Python3 – V

The default on OS X is that Python 3 is not going to be installed at all. If you want to use Python 3, you can install it using some of the installers that are on Python.org.

This is a good place to go because it will install everything that you need to write and execute your codes with Python. It will have the Python shell, the IDLE development tools, and the interpreter. Unlike what happens with Python 2.X, these tools are installed as a standard application in the Applications folder.

Being able to run the IDLE and the Python shell is going to be dependent on which version you choose and some of your own personal preferences. You can use the following commands to help you start the shell and IDLE applications:

- For Python 2.X just type in "Idle"
- For Python 3.X, just type in "idle3"

As we brought up a bit before, when you take the time to download and install Python 3, you will be able to install the IDLE in your Applications folder. Doing all of this from the Python website, www.python.org, is the best option because it will ensure that you have the right files and more that are needed to complete this process.

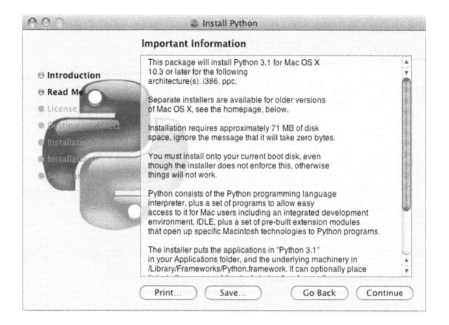

Install Python

The image above is a good one for us to work with because it shows us an example of the pup-ups that we are going to see when it comes to working with installing this on Mack. You can easily click on Continue after reading through the information, and do this a few times, and it will be set up and ready to go for our needs.

The Windows Operating System

The next operating system that we need to take a look at is how to add this to the Windows system. The Windows system is a popular option to work with because it will allow you the opportunity to do a lot of neat features, and many programmers and individual users alike are going to rely on this to get their work done. One thing that we have to notice here though is if we do use the Windows system, we will have to go through the full process of downloading and installing the Python language.

The reason for this is that Windows has its own version of a coding language already installed. Because of this, it is not going to already have Python installed as well. This doesn't mean that the Python language will not work with Windows. It works fine and you won't run into any issues at all. But you do need to go through the process and actually install it on your system.

The steps that we will need to take in order to download and install Python on a Windows system will include:

1. The first step is going to include going to the official Python Page in order to download the page and then look for the installer for a Windows system. You are able to choose the version of Python you would like to work with, but most programmers are going to go with the latest version of Python 3 that is out.
    a. The default here is that the installer is going to choose a version of Python that is 32-bit. There is an option for the 64-bit as well so you can change this if you would like.

2. After you are done with this part, you are able to right-click on your installer to get things going, and then select that you would like to Run as Administrator at this part. There

are going to just be two options for you to choose from. Our choice here is to go with Customize Installation.

3. When you click on that to start the installation, you are going to end up on the following screen with a lot of options. You want to make sure that all of the boxes under "Optional Features" are clicked, and then you can move on.

4. While you are still under the category for the Advanced Options, you will be able to pick out the best location for you to have the Python language installed on your computer. Click on Install from here. This is going to take a few moments for the installation to happen so give it some time and then close the installer.

5. Next, we need to go through the process that is needed to set the PATH variable for the system so that it is going to include all of the directories that we need. This is going to include any packages and other components that we will need later.

There are a number of steps that we are able to use for this one including:

a. The first step to work on here is to open up our Control Panel in Windows. The way that we can do this is to click on our taskbar, type in the words

"Control Panel" and then click on the icon that shows up.

b. Inside of this Control panel when it opens up, we want to do a search for the Environment. Then click on the Edit the System Environment Variables. From here, we are going to be able to click on the button for Environment Variables.

c. Go to the section that is marked for the User Variables. You get two options to work with here. You are able to create one of your own variables, or you can make some edits to the PATH variable that is there.

d. If there isn't already a variable that is present for PATH on your system, then you will need to go through this and create one. We can start this by clicking on New. Make the name for the PATH variable anything that you would like and what you can remember and add in the necessary directories that you want. Click on close so that you are out of the dialogs of this and go to the last step.

Now that you are at this part, we are able to open up the command prompt. We can do this by clicking on our Start Menu, then Windows System, and then the Command Prompt. From here we want to type in the word "python". This is going to help us to load up the interpreter for Python and then we are able to get started with our coding.

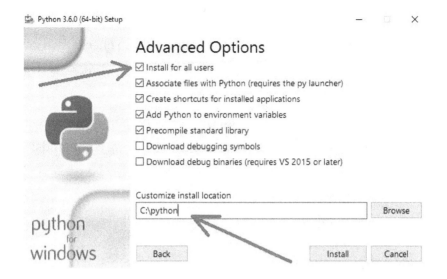

During this process, you are going to end up with a screen that asks you some of the Advanced options that you would like to use. Often you will want to leave the checks on the parts that are already there, but you do not need to do this though. You can change up the options to fit what you need. You can also consider coming up with a customized location in order to keep this organized, and to ensure that you are going to be able to get this set up the right way. Pick a location that you will be able to remember and pull out later on.

The Linux System

And the final operating system that we need to spend some time on here is how to install Python on a Linux system. Just like with the Mac OS X we need to stop and check whether there is one of the Python 3 versions already on the computer or now. You are able to open up the command prompt that comes with this operating system, and work with the code below to check:

$ python3 - - version

If you are on Ubuntu 16.10 or newer, then it is a simple process to install Python 3.6. you just need to use the following commands:

$ sudo apt-get update

$ sudo apt-get install Python3.6

If you are relying on an older version or Ubuntu or another version, then you may want to work with the deadsnakes PPA, or another tool, to help you download the Python 3.6 version. The code that you need to do this includes:

$ sudo apt-get install software-properties-common

$ sudo add-apt repository ppa:deadsnakes/ppa

suoda apt-get update

$ sudo apt-get install python3.6

The good news here is that if you are working with other distributions of Linux, it is likely that you already have Python 3 installed on the system. If not, you can use the distribution's package manager. And if the package of Python 3 is not recent enough, or not the right one for you, you can go through and use these same steps to help install a more recent version of Python on your computer as needed.

As we can see here, working with the Python coding language is going to be a simple process that anyone can do, and when we get it down and learn ow to make it work for our needs, we will be able to write any of the codes that we want. Most of the installation steps for any of the operating systems above are going to be simple, and then you are ready to go writing some of your own codes in the Python language.

Chapter 3: The Python Variables and Strings

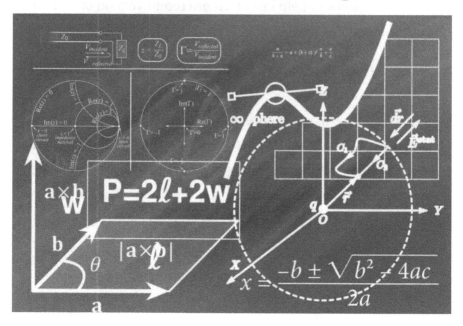

The next topic that we need to take a look at for this guidebook is the idea of the Python strings and variables. You will find that these are going to help us to keep the code going well, and will ensure that we are getting the most out of the codes that we try to write. The variables are going to help us to assign the values that we want to different parts of the code, and the strings are going to provide us with some of the text characters that we need in the code. Both of these are going to come together to help us to get some of the results that we are looking for in Python. Let's take a look at how each of these will be able to work and how we are able to make sure that this will work the way that we want.

The Python Variables

The Python variables are an important thing to work with as well. A variable, in simple terms, is often just going to be a box that we can use to hold onto the values and other things that show up in our code. They will reserve a little bit of the memory of our code so that we are able to utilize it later one. These are important because they allow us to pull out the values that we would like to use at a later time without issues along the way.

These variables are going to be a good topic to discuss because they are going to be stored inside of the memory of our code. And you will then be able to assign a value over to them, and pull them out in the code that you would like to use. These values are going to be stored in some part of the memory of your code, and will be ready to use when you need. Depending on the type of data that you will work with, the variable is going to be the part that can tell your compiler the right place to save that information to pull it out easier.

With this in mind, the first thing that we need to take a look at is how to assign a value over to the variable. To get the variable to behave in the manner that you would like, you need to make sure that a minimum of one value is assigned to it. Otherwise, you are just save an empty spot in the memory. If the variable is assigned properly to some value, and sometimes more than one value based on the code you are using, then it is going to behave in the proper manner and when you call up that variable, the right value will show up.

As you go through and work with some of the variables you have, you may find that there are three main options that are able to use. Each of these can be useful and it is often going to depend on what kind of code you would like to create on the value that you want to put with a particular variable. The three main types of variable that you are able to choose from here will include:

- Float: this would include numbers like 3.14 and so on.
- String: this is going to be like a statement where you could write out something like "Thank you for visiting my page!" or another similar phrase.
- Whole number: this would be any of the other numbers that you would use that do not have a decimal point.

When you are working with variables in your code, you need to remember that you don't need to take the time to make a declaration to save up this spot in the memory. This is automatically going to happen once you assign a value over to the variable using the equal sign. If you want to check that this is going to happen, just look to see that you added that equal sign in, and everything is going to work.

Assigning a value over to your variable is pretty easy. Some examples of how you can do this in your code would include the following:

x = 12   *#this is an example of an integer assignment*

pi = 3.14   *#this is an example of a floating point assignment*

customer name = John Doe #this is an example of a string assignment

There is another option that we are able to work with on this one, and one that we have brought up a few times within this section already. This is where we will assign more than one value to one for our variables. There are a few cases where we are going to write out our code and then we need to make sure that there are two or more values that go with the exact same variable.

To make this happen, you just need to use the same kind of procedure that we were talking about before. Of course, we need to make sure that each part is attached to the variable with an equal sign. This helps the compiler know ahead of time that these values are all going to be associated to the same variable. So, you would write out something like a = b= c= 1 to show the compiler that all of the variables are going to equal one. Or you could do something like 1 = b = 2 in order to show that there are, in this case, two values that go with one variable.

The thing that you will want to remember when you are working with these variables is that you have to assign a value in order to make the work happen in the code. These variables are also just going to be spots in your code that are going to reserve some memory for the values of your choice.

The Python Strings

The next topic that we need to take a look at in this chapter is going to be all about the strings. These strings are going to help us to learn more about how we can control some of the different parts of our codes, and will make it easier to understand what the string is. as a review, a string is just going to include a series of text characters that are found in our code for us to use.

Now, when you are working with these strings, you will find that there are some different types of operators that you are able to use when you bring them up. An operator is simply a symbol that is able to perform a specific operation that is inside of your code. When we are in this kind of situation, the operation is going to be performed on the strings. Some of the operators that you are going to be able to find here will include some of the following:

1. The concatenation operator: This is going to be the type of operator that you will use when it is time to take those strings and concatenate them.
2. Repetition operator: This is going to be the type of operator that you are able to use when you would like to get more

than one copy of your string, and often many of these copies. You are able to use this one and then choose the number of times you would like to see the string repeat.

3. Slice operator: This is going to be an operator that will take a look through the chosen string, and then will figure out the specific character that you would like to work with from there. Any time that we bring this one up, you will need to remember that the first character of your string is going to be zero.

4. Range slice operator: This is another operator that we are able to use because it can retrieve a range of characters out of the index, rather than just one character to you. If you would just like to have it showcase out one part, or one word, of that string, then you would need to work with this operator.

5. In operator: This operator is going to spend some time searching for a specified character in your target string. If you do have that specific character found in the string, then you will get the True answer returned to you. But if the operator is not able to find that answer in the string, then the False answer is going to be returned to you.

6. No in operator: This is the operator that will work in the opposite manner as the in operator. It is going to search for a specified character in your string. But if the operator is not able to find that character in the string, then you will get the True answer returned. If that character is found in the string, then it is going to return False.

As we are working on some of the strings that we want to handle, you will find that there are a lot of options that are going to be available for you to use at any time. these strings come with a lot of functions and will help you to add more options and features to some of the codes that you are trying to write. Some of the different functions that are going to work well when you design strings in Python will include:

- Capitalize(): This one is going to take the first letter of the string and capitalize it for you.
- Center(width, char): This is going to return to you a string that is at least the specified width and then it will be created by padding the string with the character.
- Count(str): This is going to return the number of times that a particular string is contained in another string.
- Find(str): This is going to return the index number of the substring in the string.
- Isalpha(): This is going to check if all the characters of a string are alphabetic characters.
- Isdigit(): This part is going to check whether the string contains just numbers or digits or if there is a mixture.
- Islower): This function is going to take a look to see if the string you are checking has all lower case characters.
- Len(): This is going to let you know the length of the string
- Isupper(): This one is going to check to see if all the characters in the string are upper case.
- Lower(): This will give you a return that has all the string in lower case letters.

- Replace(): This is going to take the string that you have and replace it with a new string
- Upper(): This is going to return the string in upper case.
- Split(): This is going to split up the string based on the split character.

Chapter 4: Handling Python Operators, Tuples, and Lists

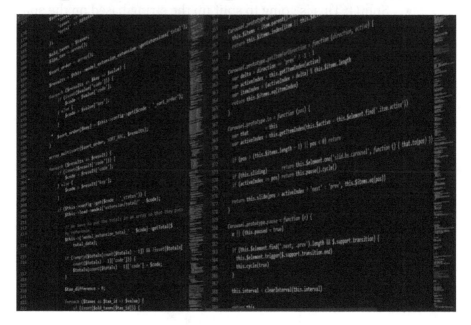

This chapter is going to take some time to delve into a few of the other parts that we need to know when it is time to work with the Python language. In this chapter, we are going to spend our time looking at how to work with the operators, as well as what the similarities and the differences between tuples and lists are. Let's dive in and learn more about these topics and how you can make them work for your needs.

The Python Operators

The Python operators are going to be pretty diverse and can do a lot of different things in your code based on how you use them. When we are talking about the operators, there are going to be quite a few different types that you are able to work with in the code. Let's explore a bit more about these operators and how we are able to use these for our needs as well.

Arithmetic Operators

The first type of operator that we are going to take a look at is the arithmetic operators. These are going to be similar to the signals and signs that we would use when we do mathematical equations. You can work with the addition, subtraction, multiplication, and division symbols in order to do the same kinds of actions on the different parts of the code that you are working with. These are common when you want to do something like add two parts of the code together with one another.

You have the freedom to add in as many of these to your code as you would like, and you can even put more than one type in the same statement. Just remember that you need to work with the rules of operation and do these in the right order in order to make it work the way that you would like. Otherwise, you will be able to add in as many of these to the same code as you need to make it work.

Operator	Description	Exam
+	Adds two operands	A + B
-	Subtracts second operand from the first	A - B
*	Multiply both operands	A * B
/	Divide numerator by denumerator	B / A
%	Modulus Operator and remainder of after an integer division	B % A
++	Increment operator, increases integer value by one	A++
--	Decrement operator, decreases integer value by one	A-- w

The above is going to be some of the different operators that you are able to work with that fit into this category. Working with these will ensure that we are able to handle the work, and that we will be able to use inside of our codes.

Comparison Operators

After looking at the arithmetic operators, it is also possible for us to work with the comparison operators. These comparison operators are going to be good to work with because they will let you take over two, and sometimes more, values and statements in the code and then see how they are going to compare to one another. This is one that we will use often for a lot of codes that are going to rely on Boolean expressions because it ensures that the answer you get back with be false and true. So your statements in this situation are going to be the same as each other, or they will be different.

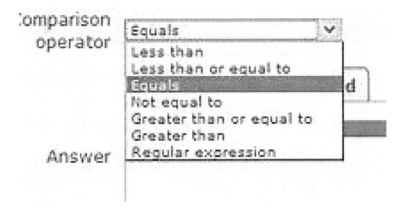

Comparison operator

Equals

Less than
Less than or equal to
Equals
Not equal to
Greater than or equal to
Greater than
Regular expression

Answer

There are a lot of times when we are going to be able to work with these comparison operators to get the most out of the programming that we are doing. You need to consider these ahead of time and make sure that we are going to be able to get the results that we need in our code.

Logical Operators

Next we are going to be looking at the logical operators. These may not be used as often as the other options, but it is still some time for us to look it over. These operators are going to be used when it is time to evaluate the input that a user is able to present to us, with any of the conditions that you are able to set in your code. There are going to be three types of logical operators that we are able to work with, and some of the examples that you are going to use in order to work with this in your code includes:

- Or: with this one, the compiler is going to evalue x and if it is false, it will then go over and evaluate y. If x ends up being true, the compiler is going to return the evaluation of x.

- And: if x ends up being the one that is fase, the compiler is going to evaluate it. If x ends up being true, it will move on and evaluate y.
- Not: if ends up being false, the compiler is going to return True. But if x ends up being true, the program will return false.

A	B	A AND B	A OR B	NO
False	False	False	False	True
False	True	False	True	True
True	False	False	True	Fals
True	True	True	True	Fals

The chart above is going to show us a bit more about the logical operators that we are able to work with as well. This can give us a good idea of what is going to happen when we use each of the operators for our own needs as well.

Assignment Operators

And the final type of operator that we are going to take a look at is the assignment operator. This is going to be the kind of operator that will show up, and if you take a look at some of the different codes that we have already taken a look at in this guidebook, you will be able to see them quite a bit. This is because the assignment operator is simply going to be an equal sign, where you will assign a value over to a variable throughout the code.

So, if you are looking to assign the number 100 over to one of your variables, you would just need to put the equal sign there between them. This can be used with any kind of variable and value that you are using in your code, and you should already have some familiarity with getting this done ahead of time. It is also possible for you to go through and take several values, assigning them to the same variable if that is best for your code. As long as you have this assignment operator, or the equal sign, in between it, you will be able to add in as many values over to the variable that you would like.

Working with these operators is a simple thing to work with, but you will find that they show up in your coding on a regular basis. You are able to use them to add your variables together, to use other mathematical operators, to assign a value over to the variable, or even a few values to your same variable. And you are able to even take these operators to compare two or more parts of the code at the same time and see I they are the same or not. As we can already see, there are so many things that we will be able to do when it comes to using these operators.

Understanding Tuples and Lists

One thing that you will see on a regular basis when you are working with the Python language is that there seems to be a big difference between the lists and the tuples that you will see with this kind of coding language. These are going to seem similar, but there are some differences that we need to be aware about, and learning what these are, and how we can work with them, can make a difference in the kinds of codes that we can write.

The Lists

To keep it easy, we are going to start with a list. A list is basically going to be a collection of objects that are kind of arbitrary, somewhat akin to what we are going to see as an array in other languages of coding, but there will be more flexibility that comes with it. Lists are going to be defined when we are able to enclose them off with a comma-separated sequence of objects in some square brackets. There are a few different characteristics that we are going to see in these Python lists, and they will include:

1. The lists are going to be ordered
2. Lists are going to be dynamic
3. Lists are going to be mutable
4. Lists can be nested to be nested to an arbitrary depth
5. The elements that are part of the list can be accessed by the index.
6. Lists are going to contain some objects that are a bit arbitrary.

The Tuples

With this in mind, we then need to take a look at what the Python tuple is going to be about. Python is going to provide us with another type that is going to be an ordered collection of objects that we are able to call a tuple. Tuples are going to be pretty similar to the lists that we already talked about, but there are a few properties that make them different.

These will include:

1. Tuples are going to be defined by enclosing the elements in parentheses instead of a square bracket.
2. The tuple is going to be immutable.

This is going to bring out one more question that we need to explore. When would we use a list, and when would it be better in our code to work with a list like we talked about before. There are benefits and negatives to each one, and often it is going to depend on what you want to see happen in the code. Some of the reasons why you would want to use a tuple instead of a list is going to include the following:

1. The tuple will allow for a faster execution of the program when you are using a tuple than it is for an equivalent list. This is not going to be as noticeable when your tuple or list

is small, but it is something to consider when you have a longer list or tuple.

2. Sometimes you do not want to make it in your code for the data to receive any modifications. If the values in the collection are going to remain constant for the life of the program, then using a tuple instead o a list is going to guard against modifications that could happen on accident.

3. There is also another type of data that we are able to explore in here a bit, and that we will look at a bit more as we go through this guidebook, known as a dictionary. This dictionary is going to require, as one of the components, a value that is immutable. A tuple can be used for this kind of purpose, while a list can't.

Working with the Python programming language and understanding when the different parts are going to come into play, including the differences between lists and tuples and the other parts of this coding language in order to write some of the codes that you are looking for overall.

Chapter 5: The Python Functions

When you are working with a language like Python, there will be times when you will need to work with something that is known as a function. These functions are going to be blocks of reusable code that you will use in order to get your specific tasks done. But when you define one of these functions in Python, we need to have a good idea of the two main types of functions that can be used, and how each of them works. The two types of functions that are available here are known as built-in and user-defined.

The built-in functions are the ones that will come automatically with some of the packages and libraries that are available in Python, but we are going to spend our time working with the user-defined functions because these are the ones that the developer will create and use for special codes they write. In Python though, one thing to remember no matter what kind of function you are working with is that all of them will be treated like objects. This is good news because it can make it a lot easier to work with these functions compared to what we may see with some other coding languages.

		Built-in Functions		
abs()	divmod()	input()	open()	staticmethod()
all()	enumerate()	int()	ord()	str()
any()	eval()	isinstance()	pow()	sum()
basestring()	execfile()	issubclass()	print()	super()
bin()	file()	iter()	property()	tuple()
bool()	filter()	len()	range()	type()
bytearray()	float()	list()	raw_input()	unichr()
callable()	format()	locals()	reduce()	unicode()
chr()	frozenset()	long()	reload()	vars()
classmethod()	getattr()	map()	repr()	xrange()
cmp()	globals()	max()	reversed()	zip()
compile()	hasattr()	memoryview()	round()	__import__()
complex()	hash()	min()	set()	
delattr()	help()	next()	setattr()	
dict()	hex()	object()	slice()	
dir()	id()	oct()	sorted()	

The user-defined functions that we are going to talk about in the next section are going to be important, and can really expand out some of the work that we are doing as well. But we also need to take a look at some of the work that we are able to do with our built-in functions as well. The list above includes many of the ones that are found inside of the Python language. Take some time to study them and see what they are able to do to help us get things done.

Why are User Defined Functions So Important?

To keep it simple, a developer is going to have the option of either writing out some of their own functions, known as a user-defined function, or they are able to go through and borrow a function from another library, one that may not be directly associated with Python. These functions are sometimes going to provide us with a few advantages depending on how and when we would like to use them in the code. Some of the things that we need to remember when working on these user-defined functions, and to gain a better understanding of how they work, will include:

- These functions are going to be made out of code blocks that are reusable. It is necessary to only write them out once and then you can use them as many times as you need in the code. You can even take that user-defined function and use it in some of your other applications as well.
- These functions can also be very useful. You can use them to help with anything that you want from writing out specific logic in business to working on common utilities. You can also modify them based on your own requirements to make the program work properly.
- The code is often going to be friendly for developers, easy to maintain, and well-organized all at once. This means that you are able to support the approach for modular design.

- You are able to write out these types of functions independently. And the tasks of your project can be distributed for rapid application development if needed.
- A user-defined function that is thoughtfully and well-defined can help ease the process for the development of an application.

Now that we know a little bit more about the basics of a user-defined function, it is time to look at some of the different arguments that can come with these functions before moving on to some of the codes that you can use with this kind of function.

Options for Function Arguments

Any time that you are ready to work with these kinds of functions in your code, you will find that they have the ability to work with four types of arguments. These arguments and the meanings behind them are something that will be pre-defined, and the developer is not always going to be able to change them up. Instead, the developer is going to have the option to use them, but follow the rules that are there with them. You do get the option to add a bit to the rules to make the functions work the way that you want. As we said before, there are four argument types you can work with and these include:

1. Default arguments: In Python, we are going to find that there is a bit different way to represent the default values

and the syntax for the arguments of your functions. These default values are going to be the part that indicates that the argument of the function is going to take that value if you don't have a value for the argument that can pass through the call of the function. The best way to figure out where the default value is will be to look for the equal sign.

2. Required argument: The next type of argument is going to be the required arguments. These are the kinds of arguments that will be mandatory to the function that you are working on. These values need to go through and be passed in the right order and number when the function is called out, or the code won't be able to run the right way.

3. Keyword arguments: These are going to be the argument that will be able to help with the function call inside of Python. These keywords are going to be the ones that we mention through the function call, along with some of the values that will go all through this one. These keywords will be mapped with the function argument so that you are able to identify all of the values, even if you don't keep the order the same when the code is called.

4. Variable arguments: The last argument that we are going to take a look at here is the variable number of arguments. This is a good one to work with when you are not sure how many arguments are going to be necessary for the code that you are writing to pass the function. Or you can use this to design your code where any number of arguments can be passed, as long as they have been able to pass any of the requirements in the code that you set.

Writing a Function

Now that we have a little better idea of what these functions are like and some of the argument types that are available in Python, it is time for us to learn the steps that you need to accomplish all of this. There are going to be four basic steps that we are able to use to make all of this happen, and it is really up to the programmer how difficult or simple you would like this to be. We will start out with some of the basics, and then you can go through and make some adjustments as needed. Some of the steps that we need to take in order to write out our own user-defined functions include:

1. Declare your function. You will need to use the "def" keyword and then have the name of the function come right after it.
2. Write out the arguments. These need to be inside the two parentheses of the function. End this declaration with a colon to keep up with the proper writing protocol in this language.
3. Add in the statements that the program is supposed to execute at this time.
4. End the function. You can choose whether you would like to do it with a return statement or not.

An example of the syntax that you would use when you want to make one of your own user-defined functions includes:

```
def userDefFunction (arg1, arg2, arg3, ...):

    program statement1

    program statement2

    program statement3

    ....

    Return;
```

Working with functions can be a great way to ensure that your code is going to behave the way that you would like. Making sure that you get it set up in the proper manner, and that you are able to work through these functions, getting them set up in the manner that you would like, can be really important as well. There are many times when the functions will come out and serve some purpose, so taking the time now to learn how to use them can be very important to the success of your code.

Chapter 6: Python as an OOP Language and Working with the Python Classes

One thing that you will notice as an important part of the Python program is that it is divided up into classes. This is going to allow you a great method to work with in Python because it can help you to organize the code that you have, and keep everything in order as much as possible. The neat thing about Python is that it works with these classes, and allows you a chance to make easy to use codes that are able to work well without all of the mess and complications that come with some of the other coding languages.

The classes that come with the Python language can be very important. These are going to ensure that we are going to be able to get the most out of some of the codes that we want to create, and will make it easier to ensure that there is enough organization that is going on as well. And when we use these classes as boxes that can hold onto some of he objects of our code, this will ensure that all of the parts are going to show up when they should.

The one thing that we have to remember with this is that we are able to add in any object that we would like to a class. But it needs to make sense why that object is in the class. The objects in the same class have to have something similar to one another, and it must make sense why they are in that same class together.

In Python, we are going to learn how to work with a few of our own classes, mainly because it is the organizing structure that comes with Python and will help us to add in some organization and will ensure that nothing in your code will get lost. To make one of these classes though, we need to pick out the right keywords, like what we talked about before. You can give the class any name that you would like, just make it something that you will be able to remember easily, and then ensure that it shows up in the code after the keyword you need.

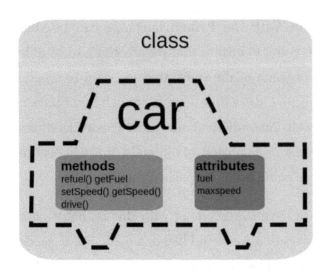

The image above is a good way to help us to learn more about how these OOP languages will work, and what we are able to do with them. We have a class of car, and then all of the methods and attributes that go with them. They all fit together inside of the class of car, even though there are a lot of different attributes that we have been able to work with, including those that are in the image and more.

After we have gone through the steps that are needed to handle our class, we also need to go through and name our own subclass. This subclass will show up in some of the parenthesis Add in the semicolon at the end to maintain some of the programming etiquette that we need.

How to Write a Class

Writing a class at this point is going to sound a bit more complicated than it needs to be. That is why we need to stop here and get a good look at an example of how this kind of coding would work with Python. Then we are able to go through a bit more later and discuss what the different parts mean, and why they are important. To start, the coding that you can use with creating your own Python class will include:

```
class Vehicle(object):

#constructor

def_init_(self, steering, wheels, clutch, breaks, gears):

self._steering = steering

self._wheels = wheels

self._clutch = clutch

self._breaks =breaks

self._gears = gears

#destructor

def_del_(self):

    print("This is destructor....")
```

#member functions or methods

def Display_Vehicle(self):

    print('Steering:' , self._steering)

    print('Wheels:', self._wheels)

    print('Clutch:', self._clutch)

    print('Breaks:', self._breaks)

    print('Gears:', self._gears)

#instantiate a vehicle option

myGenericVehicle = Vehicle('Power Steering', 4, 'Super Clutch', 'Disk Breaks', 5)

myGenericVehicle.Display_Vehicle()

If you would like, you can try out this code. Just open up your text editor and type the code inside. As you work on writing this out, you will notice that a few of the topics we have already discussed in this guidebook show up in this code. Once you have a chance to write out and then execute this code, let's divide it up and see what happened above. While we are here, we need to explore a bit about the importance of accessing the various members that come in a class. You need to set it up so that the text editor as well as your compiler are going to be able to recognize any of the classes that you would like to create. This will make it easier for them to execute the code in the proper manner. To do this, make sure that your code is set up properly.

Working with the Access Class

The good news is that there are going to be a number of methods that we are able to use in order to ensure that we can access the class members and that everything falls into place the way that we would like. The method that we are going to use though is known as the accessor method. This one is the most common that you will see, and it is going to be an efficient method to get the work done.

To help you get a better understanding of some of the ways that you can access the various members of the class that you made, we need to take a look at the following code:

class Cat(object)

   itsAge = None

   itsWeight = None

   itsName = None

   #set accessor function use to assign values to the fields or *member vars*

   def setItsAge(self, itsAge):

```python
        self.itsAge = itsAge


    def setItsWeight(self, itsWeight):

        self.itsWeight = itsWeight


    def setItsName(self, itsName):

        self.itsName =itsName

        #get accessor function use to return the values from a field

    def getItsAge(self):

        return self.itsAge

    def getItsWeight(self):

        return self.itsWeight


    def getItsName(self):

        return self.itsName


objFrisky = Cat()

objFrisky.setItsAge(5)

objFrisky.setItsWeight(10)
```

objFrisky.setItsName("Frisky")

print("Cats Name is:", objFrisky.getItsname())

print("Its age is:", objFrisky.getItsAge())

print("Its weight is:", objFrisky.getItsName())

Before we move on, type this into your compiler. If you have your compiler run this, you are going to get some results that show up on the screen right away. This will include that the cat's name is Frisky (or you can change the name to something else if you want), that the age is 5 and that the weight is 10. This is the information that was put into the code, so the compiler is going to pull them up to give you the results that you want. You can take some time to add different options into the code and see how it changes over time.

While there are a number of steps that we need to take with this kind of coding, classes are not going to be difficult to work with. These are also going to be the perfect part of the code to help you take care of the information, and keep it in order so that it is able to make more sense. You get the option o creating any kind of class that you want to work with, and fill it up with the objects that work the best for your needs.

Chapter 7: The Conditional Statements in Python

Another fun thing to work with when you are in the Python language is the conditional statements. These are going to be known by a lot of different names, such as the if statements and the decision control statements. But they are going to be a great option when you would like the program to learn how to do a few things on its own, without you having to think about all of the possible inputs before you even start.

There are going to be times when you would like to make sure that your code behaves in the right manner and can make some decisions on its own when you are not able to be there to monitor it all and hope that it all fits into the right place. Any time that you have a part of your code that will allow the user to put in any kind of answer that they want all on their own, rather than just selecting from a few options, then you are going to find that the conditional statements are the best ones to work with.

In this chapter, we are going to take a look at the three most common options of the conditional statements that you are likely to use with some of your codings. The three that we are going to focus on the most are the if statement, the if else statement, and the elif statement. These will all work in a slightly different manner from one another, but they can all add some great things to your code, so we are going to spend our time taking a look at them and how they are going to work for our needs.

The If Conditional Statements

The first thing we are going to look at is regular if statement. This keeps things simple and will ensure that we are set and ready to handle some of the basics of these conditional statements. This one is based on the idea that the answer the user gives is either true or it is false depending on what conditions you have set. If the user adds in input that the program is going to see as true, then your program will see this and will continue on to the next step. But if the user does put in an answer that is seen as false for that part of the code, then the program will just end because nothing is set up to handle this issue along the way. As we can see here already, there is the potential for some problems when you are working with this kind of coding. But we are still going to take a quick look at this to see how it works and to get the basic idea of these conditional statements, and then move on to how we can change things on to fix this issue. A good example of how the, if the statement is able to work, will be below:

```
age = int(input("Enter your age:"))

if (age <=18):

        print("You are not eligible for voting, try next election!")

print("Program ends")
```

Let's explore what is going to happen with this code when you put it into your program. If the user comes to the program and puts that they are younger than 18, then there will be a message that shows up on the screen. In this case, the message is going to say "You are not eligible for voting, try next election!" Then the program, as it is, is going to end. But what will happen to this code if the user puts in some age that is 18 or above?

With the if statement, nothing will happen if the user says that their age is above 18. The if statement just has one option and will focus on whether the answer that the user provides is going to match up with the conditions that you set with your code. The user has to put in that they are under the age of 18 with the if statement in this situation, or you won't be able to get the program to happen again.

As we have already mentioned with this one, the if statement could end up causing us a few problems when we are coding. You want to make sure that the user is able to put in any answer that is the best for them, not the "right" answer, and you want to make sure that the program you are writing is still going to be able to respond and give some kind of answer to the user along the way. Some of the users who come to your website or program will have an age that is higher than 18, and it is going to be confusing and look bad if they put that answer in and can't get the program to work.

The If Else Conditional Statement

This is why we are going to move on to the if else statement. This one is used a lot more often than we see with the if statement, and it is able to handle some of the problems that we saw with the if statement. This kind of statement is going to work with some of the topics that we had above and make some changes to fix the issues and ensure that this all works.

Let's say that we are still working with the same kind of program that we had above. But this time we want to make sure that we have some kind of result show up on the screen, no matter what answer the user inputs into our program this time. so, with this one, we are going to work to separate out the users based on their age. There will be a group who is above 18 and one that is under 18, and a response from the system based on this. The code that we would be able to use to help us write out our own if else statement is going to be below:

```
age = int(input("Enter your age:"))

if (age <=18):

        print("You are not eligible for voting, try next election!")

else

        print("Congratulations! You are eligible to vote. Check out your local polling station to find out more information!)

print("Program ends")
```

As you can see, this really helps to add some more options to your code and will ensure that you get an answer no matter what results the user gives to you. You can also change up the message to say anything that you want, but the same idea will be used no matter the answer that the user gives.

You have the option to add in some more possibilities to this. You are not limited to just two options as we have above. If this works for your program, that is just fine to use. But if you need to use more than these two options, you can expand out this as well. For example, take the option above and expand it to have several different age groups. Maybe you want to have different options come for those who are under 18, those that are between the ages of 18 and 30, and those who are over the age of 30. You can separate it out in that way and when the program gets the answer from the user, it will execute the part that you want. The cool thing with this is there are a lot of different options and programs that we are able to write that work with this. Maybe we want to create our own program that allows the user to go through and pick out one of their favorite types of candy. There are a ton of different types of candy, and they go by so many different names that it is really hard to list them all out and be prepared for this ahead of time. But the if else statement would be able to help us to handle all of this.

With this one, we would just pick out a certain number of candy choices that we would like, maybe the top six, and then list out a response that goes with that. And then we would use our else statement at the end in order to catch all of the answers that did not fit in with the original six that we listed out. This ensures that no matter what input the user adds to the system, they are going to get some kind of response out of the process as well.

The else statement in all of this is going to be an important thing to make sure it is there because it is responsible for catching all of the answers that are left that the user could potentially give to you. If you don't have this statement placed in the code, or not in the right part of the code, it is not going to be able to catch all of the other possible inputs of the user as you would like.

Now that we have had a chance to talk about the if statement and the if else statement, it is time for us to move on to our elif statements. These are a unique part of programming in the Python language, and they are going to help us add in another level to some of the conditional statements that we are able to work with. This kind of conditional statement is going to allow for a user to pick out a few choices that you present to them, and then, depending on what answer or choice the user goes with, the program is going to execute the code and provide the results that go with that answer.

The Elif Conditional Statement

You will find that these elif statements are going to show up in a lot of different places. One option is going to be when they show up in the games that you play. If you have ever gone through and played a game or been on another kind of program where you are given a menu style of choices to make, then you have already had some experience with these elif statements doing their work. These statements are a good one to work with when you would like to provide the user with some more options, rather than just limiting them to a few

When you work with this kind of elif statement, you are going to find it gives you some freedoms. You are able to choose how many statements are going to show up in this kind of code. There are no minimum or maximums as long as you go through and write out the syntax in the proper manner. You may want to make sure that you do not add in too many of these though because that can clog up the system a bit and makes it hard for the user to choose what they would like to go with.

To help us see what is going on with these elif statements and to make sure that we are going to complete the work that we need with one of these, it is good to take a look at the syntax of the elif statements to see how it works. A good example of these elif statements will include the following:

if expression1:

statement(s)

elif expression2:

statement(s)

elif expression3:

statement(s)

else:

statement(s)

This is a pretty basic syntax of the elif statement and you can add in as many of these statements as you would like. Just take that syntax and then place the right information into each part and the answer that is listed next to it. Notice that there is also an else statement at the end of this. Don't forget to add this to your code so that it can catch any answer that the user puts in that isn't listed in your elif statements.

To help you better understand how these elif statements work and how the syntax above is going to work, let's take a look at a little game that you can create using these statements:

Print("Let's enjoy a Pizza! Ok, let's go inside Pizzahut!")

print("Waiter, Please select Pizza of your choice from the menu")

pizzachoice = int(input("Please enter your choice of Pizza:"))

if pizzachoice == 1:

    print('I want to enjoy a pizza napoletana')

elif pizzachoice == 2:

    print('I want to enjoy a pizza rustica')

elif pizzachoice == 3:

    print('I want to enjoy a pizza capricciosa')

else:

    print("Sorry, I do not want any of the listed pizza's, please bring a Coca Cola for me.")

With the example above, you will find that the user is able to make some choices about what they would like to "order" from your system, and then they will click on the option that goes with this. If they want to order one of the types of pizzas, for example, they just need to click on that and will happen in the program. You can mix this up based on what you would like to see happen in the code that you are writing, but it will end up following the same basic idea in the code you are writing if you use the elif statement.

As we can see from this chapter, there are a lot of options and choices that you can go with when working on a conditional statement. They are going to provide you with a lot of power with the coding that you want to do and can make it easier for you to create some of the different kinds of codes that you would like. Make sure to take some time to explore a few of these options, and learn how you can make them work for your needs.

Chapter 8: The Python Loops

The next topic that we will need to take some time to discuss in this coding language is an idea that is known as a loop. These are going to be important to the codes that you want to write, and they can work well when you combine them with a few of the conditional statements that we talked about before. Loops are a good way to clean up your program, they can ensure that you will see a lot of work done with just a few lines of code, and it is really a great way for us to make the code intense and powerful, without having to rewrite a bunch of things or learn a lot of complicated processes.

You will find that these loops are going to be helpful when you are writing out any of the codes you want that should repeat something a number of times. This repeating needs to happen at least a few times in your code, but you want to do this without making the code messy and without having to go through and write out those lines a bunch of times either. It isn't as big of a deal to write out a few lines or write the same line two or three times. But when you think about writing out the same line of code one hundred times or more, then you can see why there is some appeal in writing loops that can handle those lines in just a few lines instead.

For example, maybe you are going through and working on your own code where you want to be able to list out the numbers from one to 50. You don't really want to spend all of your time writing that many lines of code so that the compiler can learn what it should do. When you add in a loop, you will find that it can do some of the work for you. These loops basically tell the compiler to repeat itself until you set up a condition that tells it to stop.

Multiplication Tables								
10 x 1	=	10	11 x 1	=	11	12 x 1	=	12
10 x 2	=	20	11 x 2	=	22	12 x 2	=	24
10 x 3	=	30	11 x 3	=	33	12 x 3	=	36
10 x 4	=	40	11 x 4	=	44	12 x 4	=	48
10 x 5	=	60	11 x 5	=	55	12 x 5	=	60
10 x 6	=	60	11 x 6	=	66	12 x 6	=	72
10 x 7	=	70	11 x 7	=	77	12 x 7	=	84
10 x 8	=	80	11 x 8	=	88	12 x 8	=	96
10 x 9	=	90	11 x 9	=	99	12 x 9	=	108
10 x 10	=	100	11 x 10	=	110	12 x 10	=	120
10 x 11	=	110	11 x 11	=	121	12 x 11	=	132
10 x 12	=	120	11 x 12	=	132	12 x 12	=	144

To write out a table like the one above, you have two options. You can go through and type in all of the parts one at a time. Or you can go through and use a loop and get it done in just a few lines of codes. We will take a look at the nested loop in a few pages and show you exactly how we are able to work with these loops for our needs.

While this is a process that can sometimes sound a bit complex, you will find that these loops can actually be pretty easy to work with. These loops are basically there to tell your compiler that it needs to repeat the same block of code more than one time. The compiler will continue reading through the same block of code against until the inserted condition is met and ready to be used. So, if you want to allow the code to count from one to 50, you would just tell the compiler to read through the same lines of code until the output is higher than 50. We will take a look at a few of the codes that you will be able to write out that can handle this problem for us. Of course, when writing a loop condition, you need to be careful about getting the condition set up. If you don't set up your condition from the beginning, then the program will just keep reading the code over and over again, getting stuck in a continuous loop. You need to have a condition or a break in your code to help it stop and move on to the next thing the program should do.

With the traditional methods of coding that you may have used in the past, you would have to write out every line of code. Even if there were some similar parts of code that were the same, or you were basically retyping the same piece of code over and over again, that is how you had to do it as a beginner because that is the only way that you knew how to do things.

With the help of these loops, you can get rid of that way of thinking. You can combine a lot of lines of code into just a few and instead convince the compiler to read through that same line as many times as you need. If you need it to do it 100 times, then that is what the compiler will do. With one line of code, thanks to these loops, you can get a ton of things done without having to write out 100 lines, or more, of code.

With all of this said, there are a few options that you are able to choose when it is time to try out the loops. The method that you are going to pick will depend on what you would like to see happen in the program, and even how many times you are hoping that the compiler will go through the loop at a minimum. We are going to take some time now to look at the three most popular types of loops that are likely to show up in some of the programmings that you do including the nested loop, the while loop, and the for a loop.

The While Loop

On our list, we are going to start out with the while loop. This while loop is going to be the type of loop that we will use if we would like to make sure our code will go through the cycle at least a minimum number of times. You are able to set how many times you would like the loop to happen when you are writing out the code to make sure that the loop will go through the process for as long as you need it too.

With this kind of loop in Python, your goal will not be to have the code go through a cycle an indefinite number of times, but you do want to make sure that it is able to do it a specific number of times, the amount that will ensure your code works how you would like.

Going back to our earlier example, if you want to have the program count from one to 50, you want to make sure that this program is going to head through the loop 50 times to finish it all off. With this option, the loop will go through the process a minimum of one time, and then will check out whether the conditions of that loop have been met or not. It will put up the number one, then check to see whether this output meets the conditions, see that it does not, put in the number two, and continue this loop until it sees that it is at a number that is higher than 50.

This is a simple kind of loop that we are able to work with and we are going to see how we can put it to practical use for some of the work that we want to do. To get a better idea of how we are able to get these loops to work, let's take a look at some of the sample codes of a while loop and see what is going to happen when it gets to work:

counter = 1

while(counter <= 3):

> *principal = int(input("Enter the principal amount:"))*

> *numberofyeras = int(input("Enter the number of years:"))*

> *rateofinterest = float(input("Enter the rate of interest:"))*

> *simpleinterest = principal * numberofyears * rateofinterest/100*

print("Simple interest = %.2f" %simpleinterest)

#increase the counter by 1

counter = counter + 1

print("You have calculated simple interest for 3 time!")

Before we move on, take this code and add it to your compiler and let it execute this code. You will see that when this is done, the output is going to come out in a way that the user can place any information that they want into the program. Then the program will do its computations and figure out the interest rates, as well as the final amounts, based on whatever numbers the user placed into the system. With this particular example, we set the loop up to go through three times. This allows the user to put in results three times to the system before it moves on. You can always change this around though and add in more of the loops if it works the best for your program.

Working with the For Loop

Now that we have had a chance to look at the while loop and see all of the benefits that we are able to get when working with that kind of loop, it is time for us to move on to the third type of loop that we are able to use in this kind of coding. There are times when we will need to work with a slightly different idea in some of the coding that we want to do, and this is where we will want to bring in the for loop. Many times the work that you will do with the while loop can also be done with the loop, and this loop is seen as the traditional form of working on loops so you are more likely to see this one a lot in the coding you do.

With the for loop that we are going to work with, you will find that you can set all of this up so that the user will not be the one who goes through and provides the information to the loop on when it should stop. Instead, the loop will be set up to go over the iteration in the order that things are going to show up in the statement that you write, and then this information is the kind that will show up on the screen. With this one, you will be noticed that there isn't really going to be much of a need for input from any outside force or even from the user, at least until your loop is done and reaches the end.

A good example of working with the for loop is going to include:

Measure some strings:

words = ['apple', 'mango', 'banana', 'orange']

for w in words:

print(w, len(w))

When you work with the for loop example that is above, you are able to add it to your compiler and see what happens when it gets executed. When you do this, the four fruits that come out on your screen will show up in the exact order that you have them written out. If you would like to have them show up in a different order, you can do that, but then you need to go back to your code and rewrite them in the right order, or your chosen order. Once you have then written out in the syntax and they are ready to be executed in the code, you can't make any changes to them.

The Nested Loop

And finally, we are going to take a look at the final type of loop, the one that is known as the nested loop. This one is going to work in a slightly different manner than we may see with the for loop and the while loop, but there are times when it can come in handy and will help us to get a lot of things done in our coding. When we do decide to work with one of the nested loops, you are basically taking one loop, and then placing it so that it goes inside of another loop. Then it is set up that both of these loops will continue to run until everything is done. This may seem like a silly thing to add to some of the codings that we do, and it may seem overly complicated for what we want to accomplish. but there are a lot of times when we will need this to show up in our codes. For example, maybe we want to create a code that is able to write out a multiplication table for us. Maybe you want to have it set up so that it can multiply from one time one all the way to ten times ten.

If you went through and wrote this out by hand, which you certainly can if you would like, this would take an enormous amount of code to get it done and to ensure the program is going to behave how you want. This is a lot of time and wasted energy though since you can easily just work with the nested loop to get it all done. This can get the work done in just a few lines of code, rather than hundreds of lines of code, and can save time. The code that you are able to use in order to create a nested loop and make your own multiplication table will include:

#write a multiplication table from 1 to 10

For x in xrange(1, 11):

    For y in xrange(1, 11):

    Print '%d = %d' % (x, y, x*x)

When you got the output of this program, it is going to look similar to this:

1*1 = 1

1*2 = 2

1*3 = 3

1*4 = 4

All the way up to 1*10 = 2

Then it would move on to do the table by twos such as this:

2*1 =2

$2*2 = 4$

And so on until you end up with $10*10 = 100$ as your final spot in the sequence.

Go ahead and put this into the compiler and see what happens. You will simply have four lines of code, and end up with a whole multiplication table that shows up on your program. Think of how many lines of code you would have to write out to get this table the traditional way that you did before? This table only took a few lines to accomplish, which shows how powerful and great the nested loop can be.

These loops are an important part of any code that you would like to write and taking the time to learn how to use them, and the different steps that you are able to use to make them work for your needs can be important as well. There are a lot of reasons that you would want to make a loop and make sure that it is added to your code. You will be able to use this as a method to get a ton of coding done, and rather than taking up a lot of time and lines and making your code look messy, you can clean it up with one of the three loops above.

Chapter 9: Handling Your Own Exceptions

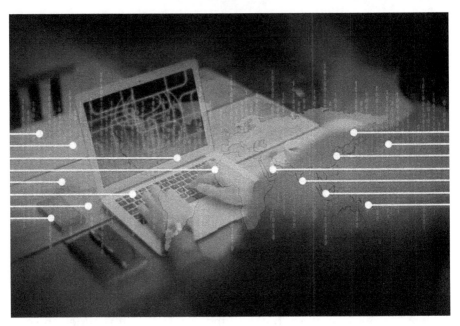

Another great thing that we are able to do when it comes to working with our Python language is known as exception handling. This is going to be a unique topic that we are going to spend a little bit of time on here because of its importance, but in the beginning, it is going to sound a little bit confusing. Don't worry though because you will catch on quickly, and it won't be long before you are able to raise an exception, make changes to the exception, and even create some of your own exceptions that will be unique to the code that you are working with.

As you are going through some of the work that you need to handle in your code, you may find that there are going to be a few exceptions that the program is already going to bring out for you. And then there are also going to be a few that you will want to write on your own to ensure that the program is going to work the way that you would like. You will be able to find some of the automatic ones already in the standard library for Python. A good example of this is when you or the user will try to divide by zero in the code. The Python language will automatically not allow this to happen, so it is going to raise one of these exceptions for it. But if there is a special kind of exception that you want to work with when you are working on your own codes, and you will be able to add this in as well.

Now, the first part of this process is to raise an exception that the compiler will be able to recognize because of the standard library of Python. If the user does one of the things that will automatically bring it up the way that we want. This could be something simple like using an improper statement in our code, or misspelling one of our classes so that the computer is not sure what you are looking for when you try to search or it at another time. These are things that the compiler is going to see as errors already, and you will need to go through and learn how to handle these.

As a programmer, it is going to be your job, and a good idea, to know some of the kinds of exceptions that are going to be found in this kind of standard library with Python. This is going to be helpful to work with because it is going to tell us what to add into our codes, and when an exception is going to turn up for you.

Some of the exceptions that the standard library of Python will already know about, and the different keywords that we need to be aware of will include:

- Finally—this is the action that you will want to use to perform cleanup actions, whether the exceptions occur or not.
- Assert—this condition is going to trigger the exception inside of the code
- Raise—the raise command is going to trigger an exception manually inside of the code.
- Try/except—this is when you want to try out a block of code and then it is recovered thanks to the exceptions that either you or the Python code raised.

How to Raise An Exception

The first thing that we are going to take a look at here is how to raise up an exception inside of your code. We are going to work with some of the automatic ones that are going to show up. When you see these, you want to make sure that you are prepared and that you know what you are able to do to handle these, and ensure that they are easier to work with and understand.

If you are working on a new code and you notice that there is a potential kind of issue that is showing up, or you want to go through the steps and figure out why your program is doing something that seems a bit off, then you may be able to check with the compiler and see that at this time, it is raising up a new exception for you. This is due to the fact that your program ran a bit, had a chance to take a look through the code, and found that it was not able to proceed. You then have to go through and check it out to figure out what is wrong and how you can fix this kind of issue. The good thing to remember here is that many times the issues you are dealing with will be simple, and you will be able to fix them pretty easily. For example, if you are going through your code and trying to bring up a file, and you provided it with the wrong name, either when you first named it or when it was time to call it up, your compiler is going to go through and raise a new exception. The program took the time to look through your code and noticed that there was stuff going on that it was not able to help you out with at all, and so it raised this exception.

A good way for you to really get into some of these exceptions and see how they work is to actually take some time to write out your own examples and get some practice with them. This helps us to see what is going to happen when the compiler is able to raise up one of the exceptions. The code that you are able to use in order to see what happens with your compiler when you do it is going to be below:

$x = 10$

$y = 10$

$result = x/y$ #trying to divide by zero

print(result)

The output that you are going to get when you try to get the interpreter to go through this code would be:

>>>

Traceback (most recent call last):

    File "D: \Python34\tt.py", line 3, in <module>

    result = x/y

ZeroDivisionError: division by zero

>>>

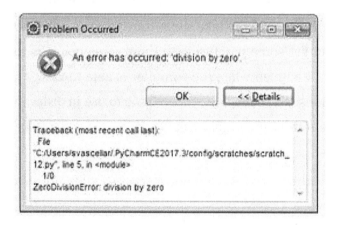

The picture above is going to be a good example of what is going to show up when we try to divide by zero. We are able to change up the message to make it work with what we should see within the code.

When you take a look at this example, your compiler is going to bring up an error, simply because you or the user is trying to divide by zero. This is not allowed with the Python code so it will raise up that error. Now, if you leave it this way and you run the program exactly how it is, you are going to get a messy error message showing up, something that your user probably won't be able to understand. It makes the code hard to understand, and no one will know what to do next. A better idea is to look at some of the different options that you can add to your code to help prevent some of the mess from before. You want to make sure that the user understands why this exception is being raised, rather than leaving them confused in the process. A different way that you can write out this code to make sure that everyone is on the same page includes:

x = 10

y = 0

result = 0

try:

    result = x/y

    print(result)

except ZeroDivisionError:

   print("You are trying to divide by zero.")

As you can see, the code that we just put into the compiler is going to be pretty similar to the one that we wrote above. But we did go through and change up the message to show something their when the user raises this exception. When they do get this exception, they will see the message "You are trying to divide by zero" come up on the screen. This isn't a necessary step, but it definitely makes your code easier to use!

How to Define My Own Exceptions

The next thing that we need to take a look at is some of the steps that we are able to use in order to raise our own exceptions. With the work that we did above, we spent our time handling any of the automatic exceptions that were found by the program and that the standard library of Python was going to recognize. Then we went a bit further and found out some of the steps that we are able to use in order to personalize the message that comes with that exception, rather than just leaving it in an automatic manner that most non-programmers, or your regular users, are not going to understand.

Now that we have that out of the way, it is time for us to take our exception writing skills to the next level, and really learn how we can write some of our own exceptions to fit the kinds of codes that we are writing. This is not going to come into play all of the time, but sometimes it can really be helpful in make sure you are going to get everything done the way that you would like.

For example, maybe you are working on some new program or code, and you want to set it up so that your users are only going to be able to add in input of certain numbers, and then not allow some of the other numbers. Or you could have an exception that will show up when the user tries to guess more than three times. These are both things that could come up in a game, and having the process set up to handle these, and raising some of your own exceptions can make a big difference.

Keep in mind with some of these kinds of exceptions that they are unique to the program that you are creating. If you don't specifically add these exceptions into the mix, then the compiler won't recognize that there is anything wrong here, and will just keep going. You are able to add in as many of these exceptions, and any kind of exception that you would like, and it is going to follow a fairly similar idea to what we say before. The code that we are going to use to ensure that this happens the way that we want though will include:

class CustomException(Exception):

def_init_(self, value):

> *self.parameter = value*

def_str_(self):

return repr(self.parameter)

try:

    raise CustomException("This is a CustomError!")

except CustomException as ex:

    print("Caught:", ex.parameter)

When you finish this particular code, you are done successfully adding in your own exception. When someone does raise this exception, the message "Caught: This is a CustomError!" will come up on the screen. You can always change the message to show whatever you would like, but this was there as a placeholder to show what we are doing. Take a moment here to add this to the compiler and see what happens.

There are a lot of different times when you will want to work with exception handling. This is something that we are going to focus on more and more when we bring in some of the advanced types of codes that are possible with Python. There are many times that you can work with both types of exceptions that were discussed in this chapter, and you will find that they are going to help you to get more done overall. Make sure to practice some of the codes above to make sure that you have exception handling down and ready to go.

Chapter 10: Python Encapsulation

The next topic that we need to take some time to learn about in this guidebook is the idea of data encapsulation. This is going to refer to the process of sending data. And we want to send this data where the data is augmented with successive layers of control information before it is transmitted to go across the network. The reverse that we are going to see with this kind of encapsulation is going to be known as decapsulation, which is when we refer to those successive layers from before being removed, or unwrapped, at the receiving end of the network. To

When you are working on coding, the variable of your object is not always going to be something that you can access directly. To prevent there being an accidental change, the variable of an object can sometimes only be changed in certain situations, such as with the method or methods of those objects. These variables are going to be known as private variables.

The methods that are there to ensure the correct values are set are important. If you have an incorrect value that have been set then this kind of method is going to return an error to you. You will find that while working with the encapsulation idea, Python is not going to come with a private keyword. This is a little bit different than what we are going to find with some of the other object-oriented programming languages that are out there. this doesn't mean that you are lost though. You will be able to go through and use the process of encapsulation in order to get the work done. It is also important to learn a bit about the differences between encapsulation and abstraction. With abstraction, which is a similar idea, we are using a mechanism that is going to represent all of the essential features of that part of the code, without having to include any of the implementation details. With abstraction, we are hiding the implementation. With encapsulation, we are trying to hide the information.

Python is going to follow the idea that we're all adults when it comes to hiding the methods and the attributes that are in our codes. What this means is that we need to place some trust in the other programmers who go through and try to use any of your classes. You need to stick with some of the plain attributes as much as possible because these are easier to work with, and can make sure that your code has fewer problems in the long run.

The Getter and Setter

Now, as you go through with this, it is tempting to use the getter and setter methods that you want to use, rather than the attributes. But for the most part, the only time that you will want to use the getters and the setters is to make sure that you can change up the implementation a bit later on if it is needed. However, you will find that with some of the newer versions of Python, including Python2.2 and later will allow doing certain things with properties:

1. Protected members: Protected members will be those that are only going to be accessible only from within the class and all of the subclasses. This is something that we are going to see with Java and C++ quite a bit. How are we going to be able to accomplish this in Python though? This is done by a process known as the convention. When we are able to prefix the name of a member with just one underscore, we are basically telling others that we don't want it to be touched, unless it is going to be a subclass that is there.

2. Private members: In addition to working with some of the protected members, we are also going to work with the private members. There is going to be a method in Python that is used to define private that has a double underscore that is in front of the function and the variable name. this is

going to be the right way to hide these when you would like to try and access them from outside of the class.

a. Remember here that the Python language is not going to have a real private method, so one underline that shows up at the beginning of the attribute or the method means that you should not be able to access the method. But this is going to be a convention, and it is still possible for us to access the variable with the use of just one underscore. In addition, we are still able to access the private variables even when we bring in the double underscore.

Putting It All Together

Let's take a quick look at how this is going to work with our class. Remember that we talked about the private members with some of our coding above, but let's look at an example of how we are able to access this private member data with the help of a process that is known as name mangling. The process that we will use to make this happen includes:

```
class Person:
def __init__(self):
self.name = 'Manjula'
self.__lastname = 'Dube'
```

```
def PrintName(self):
return self.name +'' + self.__lastname

#Outside class
P = Person()print(P.name)
print(P.PrintName())
print(P.__lastname)
#AttributeError: 'Person' object has no attribute '__lastname'
```

As we can see already, there are a lot of differences from what we are going to see with encapsulation and data hiding within the Python language. This is especially true when we compare this process to some of the work that we are able to do with other coding languages as well. But there are still some methods that we are able to do around this in order to get some of the results that we are looking for in the process.

With Python, instead of working with the private keyword, you are going to rely on the convention: a class variable that should not be accessed directly is going to be prefixed with the help of an underscore. If you have worked with some of the other coding languages in the past, you will find that it is going to be a bit harder to work with and can take you some time to see results. But the good news is that if this is the first coding language that you are working with, it is not going to take up much more of your effort and it can be easier for you to work with. The coding that you are able to do to make this happen includes:

```
lass Robot(object):
  def __init__(self):
    self.a = 123
    self._b = 123
    self.__c = 123

obj = Robot()
print(obj.a)
print(obj._b)
print(obj.__c)
```

Take some time to add this to your compiler and run it to see what is going to happen. You may then find that there is going to be an error and an underscore that shows up. When we end up with a single underscore, this means that we are working with a private variable. This means that you do not want to access it directly. But nothing is going to stop you from doing this, except the convention.

Then we are going to work with a double underscore. This is going to be a private variable. This is going to make it a bit harder to reach that particular variable, but it is still possible in some cases. Remember that both are going to be accessible in some cases. Python is going to have some private variables by convention, but you still need to be careful about what is able to reach which part throughout this process.

While we are on this process, we need to spend a few minutes talking about the getters and the setters. The private variables are intended to be changed with the methods that are known as getter and setter. You are able to use these to provide some indirect access to your private variables. An example of how you would be able to go through and write out this kind of code would include:

```
class Robot(object):
  def __init__(self):
    self.__version = 22

  def getVersion(self):
    print(self.__version)

  def setVersion(self, version):
    self.__version = version

obj = Robot()
obj.getVersion()
obj.setVersion(23)
obj.getVersion()
print(obj.__version)
```

The values with this method will be changed inside of the class methods that you are working with. This is a simple example of what we are able to work with, but we are able to go through and do some additional checks if we would like to. For example, one of the checks that you will want to do is see whether or not the value is too large or not negative based on your own conditions.

What to Keep In Mind

As you go through this process, there are a number of things that we need to keep in mind when it is time to access the private functions or the private members that we want to work within this language.

Some of the things that we need to keep track of when we work in this language by accessing the parts that we want to keep private will   include:

1. When you write out one of the attributes that need to go with an object, and that attribute does not exist, the system of Python is not going to send up an error or complain about this. Instead, it is just going to go through and create a brand new attribute for you to use.
2. Private attributes are not ones that the Python system is going to protect. This was a design decision that you will work with.
3. For the most part, the private attributes that you want to work with are going to be masked. The reason for this is that there should never be a clash that happens in the inheritance chain. The masking is going to be done by

some implicit renaming throughout the code. Private attributes will still need to come with a real name.

Chapter 11: Python Databases & Dictionaries and How to Work with Them

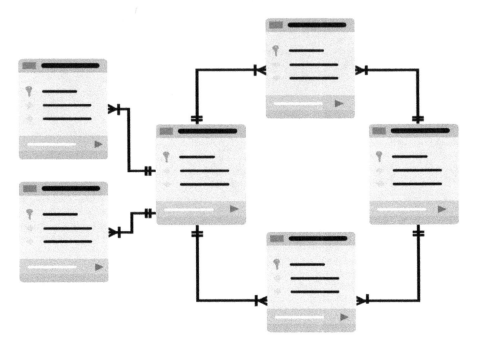

The databases and the dictionaries that are found in the Python language are going to be important parts of coding in this kind of language. When we are able to use this in the proper manner, we will be able to search and use the data that we want, and we will find that the dictionaries will be able to help us out with some of the extra features and more that we need to work with inside of this kind of language.

When we are able to combine these together we have the features and more that are needed to keep our codes as strong as possible. Let's dive into both of these and see what we are able to do with the Python databases and Python dictionaries.

The Python Database

There are a number of databases that are going to work well when we want to make sure that the Python language is going to work the way that we want. We have to make sure that we know what these databases are capable of, and that we are able to use them in the proper manner and more.

There are many times when the Python language is going to rely on these databases. This becomes even more apparent when we are working on things like data science and machine learning. Being able to work with these databases will make a world of difference, and can help us to gather up, and analyze some of the different types of data that we need to complete these processes. The good news is that there are a lot of different options that we are able to bring out when it is time to work with the databases in Python, and some of these will include:

1. DB-API: The Python Database API is going to be useful because it is going to define a standard kind of interface for the Python database access modules. Nearly all of the

modules for Python databases are going to conform to this kind of interface in some manner.

2. SQLAlchemy: This is going to be a very commonly used toolkit for a database that you are able to use. Unlike some of the other libraries, it not only provides us with an ORM layer to work with, but it can provide us with a generalized API for helping us to write out database-agnostic code without SQL being present.

3. Records: Records are another choice that you can make that is an SQL library that is minimalistic. You will find that this one is designed for sending out some raw SQL queries for various databases. Data can be used programmatically or we are able to export to a number of useful data formats overall.

4. PlugSQL: This is another simple interface for Python to help organize and using the parameterized and handwritten form of SQL. It is going to be an anti-ORM that will be lo-fi for the most part, but it is still going to present a nice, simple, and clean interface in Python.

5. Django ORM: This is going to be the interface with Python that is going to be used by Django in order to provide us with some access to the database. It is going to be based on

the ideas of models, and abstraction that is going to make it a bit easier to manipulate the data you have in Python. The basics of this one will include:

    a. Each model is going to be a Python class that is going to subclass the djgano.db.models.Model

    b. Each attribute of the model is going to represent a field in the database.

    c. Django is going to give you some database access to the API to make queries that are automatically generated.

6. Peewee: This is another type of ORM that will focus on being a lightweight version that provides us with support for Python 2.6+ and 3.2+. It is also going to, by default, help us support PostgreSQL, MySQL, and SQLite. The model layer is going to be similar to find with Django ORM, and it is going to have a few methods to help us query the data.

7. PonyORM: This is going to be a different kind of ORM that focuses on a different approach in order to query the database. Instead of writing out the work in a Boolean expression or an SQL-like language, the generator syntax of Python is going to be used. There is also a graphical schema editor that is able to generate the PonyORM entities for you.

8. SQLObject: The final thing that we are going to take a look at here is working with the database known as SQLObject. This one is able to support a wide variety of databases to help you get your work done and it works with some of the newer versions of Python as well.

As we can see here, there are a lot of different databases that we are able to work with, and they can all help us to get the results that we would like in no time. When it is time to use Python to help us gather up more information about our industry and more things, then working with the database is going to be one of the best ways to do this. Make sure to focus on the database that is going to be the best for your needs.

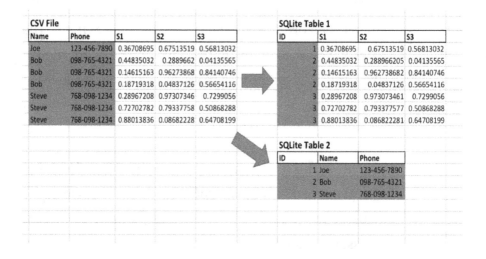

The chart above is going to give us a good look at how we are able to work with a database when we are handling some of the work that we need to do in the Python language. Taking the time to add in the entries will help us to set this all up and get it to work for things like data science and more later on.

The Python Dictionaries

Python is going to provide us another type of data that we are able to use known as a dictionary. This is going to be similar to working with a list, or a collection of objects. We are going to spend some time taking a look at some of the basic parts of a dictionary in Python, and how we are able to access and manage the data that happens in a dictionary. Once you are done, this is going to be enough to help us know when to use the dictionary, the appropriate type of data, and how to do this work as well.

There are a few things that a list and a dictionary are going to have in common, which is going to make it seem, in some cases, like you are working with the same thing. Some of the similarities that come with this include:

1. Both are going to be mutable.
2. Both the dictionary and the list will be dynamic. This means that we will be able to get them to shrink and grow as needed.
3. Both the dictionary and the list are able to be nested. A list is able to contain another list, and a dictionary will be able

to contain another dictionary. A dictionary also has the ability to contain a list and vice versa as well.

However, there are going to be a few times when the dictionary is going to differ from some of the lists that you would like to use as well. Dictionaries are going to differ, for the most part, from lists primarily in how the elements are going to be accessed overall. These include:

1. The elements of a list are going to be accessed by the position that they have on the list through the process of indexing.
2. Dictionary elements are accessed via keys.

With this in mind, we are going to take a look at how to define our own dictionary. Dictionaries are going to be the implementation of Python for a structure of data that we usually call an associative array. A dictionary is going to consist of a collection of key-value pairs.

Each of these pairs is important because they are going to map the key to its associated value. You are able to go through and define a dictionary simply by enclosing a comma-separated list of key-value pairs in the curly braces. And then you can work with a colon in order to separate out each of the keys from the value that is associated with it.

It is easy to see a lot of examples of how this is going to work in your code. We are going to add in a look at a dictionary, one that is going to define a map of a location to the name of its corresponding Major League Baseball team as well:

```
>>> MLB_team = {
...     'Colorado' : 'Rockies',
...     'Boston'  : 'Red Sox',
...     'Minnesota': 'Twins',
...     'Milwaukee': 'Brewers',
...     'Seattle' : 'Mariners'
... }
```

With this in mind, we are able to go through and create one of our own dictionaries as well. In Python, we are able to create our own dictionary by placing the sequence of elements that we want to use within curly {} braces, and then we will separate it out by a comma. Dictionary will hold a pair of values, one being the key, and then the other one is going to hold a corresponding pair element that is going to be the key: value.

Values in a dictionary can be any type of data that you would like, and you can duplicate it as much as possible. However, you need to make sure that the keys you are using are not repeatable and that you make them immutable.

```
In [12]:  #take the list of sellerID from Xvariable file
          from collections import defaultdict
          keys = ['31', '53', '57', '57', '57', '82', '82
          values = ['70803', '70901', '70801', '70801', '

          d = {}
          for k,v in zip(keys, values):
              d.setdefault(k, []).append(v)
          d

Out[12]:  {'1037': ['70803'],
           '1068': ['70803', '70803', '70805', '70805'],
           '1088': ['70803'],
           '1217': ['70809'],
           '1361': ['70804',
           '70804',
           '70804',
           '70804',
           '70804',
           '70804',
           '70804',
```

With the above, we are able to get a good look at what we are able to do when it comes to handling our own dictionaries in this language. The Python dictionaries are able to bring up a lot of the things that we are looking for when it is time to get organization and more in all of our work and coding as well.

Dictionaries are also going to be crated with the function that is already found in Python known as dict()> An empty dictionary is something that you are able to just work with that and the curly braces and that is it. Dictionary keys are going to be case sensitive. This means that you can have the same name, but different cases, with the key will still have it treated in a different manner.

With this in mind, let's take a look at how we would be able to write out some of this code to make it work for our needs. A good example of working with a few of the different things that you need for the dictionary will include:

 # Creating an empty Dictionary
Dict = {}
print("Empty Dictionary: ")
print(*Dict*)

 # Creating a Dictionary
 # with Integer Keys
Dict = {1: 'Geeks', 2: 'For', 3: 'Geeks'}
print(*"\nDictionary with the use of Integer Keys: ")*
print(*Dict*)

 # Creating a Dictionary
 # with Mixed keys
Dict = {'Name': 'Geeks', 1: [1, 2, 3, 4]}
print(*"\nDictionary with the use of Mixed Keys: ")*
print(Dict)

 # Creating a Dictionary
 # with dict() method
Dict = dict({1: 'Geeks', 2: 'For', 3:'Geeks'})
print(*"\nDictionary with the use of dict(): ")*
print(Dict)
 # Creating a Dictionary
 # with each item as a Pair
Dict = dict([(1, 'Geeks'), (2, 'For')])
print(*"\nDictionary with each item as a pair: ")*

print(Dict)

During this time, it is also possible for us to add in some elements in our dictionary. There are a number of methods that we are able to use to make this happen. For example, we can use the defining value with the key in order to just add one of the values at a time. Updating an existing value is also possible in our dictionary because we can use the method of update() to do this. In some cases, you are even able to add in some of the nested key values to this to help create an even stronger dictionary.

One thing to remember here is that when you are adding a value, which is completely acceptable in this kind of coding if the key-value already exists, then the value is going to be updated. But if the value doesn't exist when you start, then you will get a new key along with its corresponding value, to add to your dictionary.

The next thing that we can do is access the elements that we need out of the dictionary. In order to access the different items that are in the dictionary, you need to refer to the name of its key. Key can be used inside of the square brackets as well. There is also going to be the get() method that will also help us when it is time for us to access and use the element that comes from one of your dictionaries.

Looking at the process to remove elements out of the dictionary can be important as well. In this kind of dictionary, the deletion of keys can be done when you are working with the keyword of del. Using this keyword helps because it can help you to either delete specific values form the dictionary, or even the whole dictionary if you would like. There are a number of other functions that you can use as popitem() and pop() can also be used for helping us to delete the arbitrary values and the specific values from the dictionary. All the items that are in your specific dictionary can be deleted in one fell swoop if you would like with the help of the clear() method. Items in the nested dictionary can go through the process of being deleted as well with the del keyword and providing over a specific nested key and a particular key that you would like to delete out of that kind of dictionary.

Another thing to keep in mind with this is if you use the code "del Dict" it is going to end up deleting the whole dictionary. And if you go through and try to print this after the deletion, you are going to get an error as well.

There are a few different methods that we are able to use when it comes to handling the dictionary that you would like to handle. Some of the different methods that we need to focus on to help us gain the control that we want with our dictionary includes:

1. Copy(): This method is going to return for us a shallow copy of our dictionary.
2. Clear(): This method is going to help us remove all of the different items out of our dictionary.
3. Pop(): This one is going to remove and then will return an element that is in your dictionary that has the specific key that you are looking for.

4. Popitem(): This method is going to remove the arbitrary key-value pair from the dictionary, and will make sure that it is returned to you as a tuple.

5. Get(): This is going to be a conventional method that will make it easier to access the value we need with a key.

6. Dictionary_name.values(): This method is going to return a list of all the values available in a given dictionary.

7. Str(): This one is going to help us produce a printable string that is going to be a representation of our dictionary.

8. Update(): This one will add in the dictionary dict2's key-values pairs to the dictionary.

9. Keys(): When you use this method, we are going to get a list of the dictionary keys that we want to work with.

10. Items(): This one is going to return to us a list of dict's, or the key and value, in tuple pairs.

11. Has_key(): This one is going to return to us true if the key in the dictionary dict, false if not.

12. Fromkeys(): This method is going to create a new dictionary that is going to have the keys out of the seq and the values set to value.

13. Type(): This method is going to help us to return the type of the variable that we were able to pass.

14. Cmp(): This is going to help us to compare the elements of both dict.

There are a lot of times when we will want to work with the idea of a dictionary in our code, and we have already taken some time to explore how this will work, and why it is so important to some of the codes that we would like to write. Make sure to spend some time looking this over and seeing just how we are going to be able to make the dictionary work for your project.

Chapter 12: Working with GUI and CGI in This Language

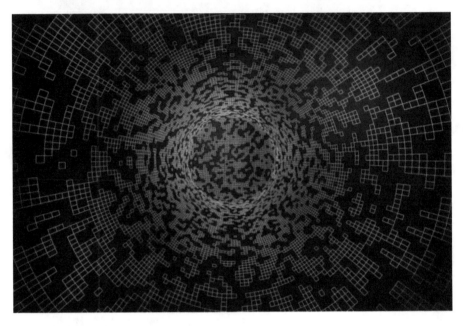

To more important parts that we need to talk about when it comes to working with the Python language is the idea of working with the GUI and the CGI of your computer. You will find that both of these are going to be things that Python is able to handle, and when we are able to put it all together, it is easier to handle some of the more complex things that we would like. So, let's dive right in and see what we are able to do with these two topics.

Getting Familiar with GUI

The first thing that we are going to take a look at here is how to work with the topic of GUI In Python. The GUI is going to stand for Graphical User Interface, and it is often going to be similar to the little different icons that we will see on our operating system that allow us to get online or into another program, without having to open up the command line and then writing that in as well. There are times when you will need to go through and write out the commands and the codes that you want to work with, but there are also going to be times when the GUI is going to be the best option that you would like to use.

Python is going to provide us with a few different options when it is time to write out some GUI based programs that work for our needs. These can include a few options like:

1. Tkinter: This is often the easiest option that we are able to work with. It is going to be the standard in Python for GUI and it is going to be used for this kind o thing the most.
2. JPython: This is going to be a Python platform for Java that is providing us with some scripts in Python that help us to get all of this done with the help of the Java language as well.
3. wxPythn: This is going to be one of the options that are bundled with Python and going to be an alternative of Tkinter as well.

Now that we know a bit more about the Tkinter program, we are going to take a look at some of the sample examples that we are able to work with here. IN this program, it is shown how Tkinter is going to be used with the help of Python in order to build up windows, and some buttons and the events that we want to have associated with these buttons as well.

The code that we are able to use for this one will include:

```
import Tkinter as tk
from Tkinter import *
from Tkinter import ttk

class karl( Frame ):
    def __init__( self ):
        tk.Frame.__init__(self)
        self.pack()
        self.master.title("Karlos")
        self.button1 = Button( self, text = "CLICK HERE", width = 25,
                    command = self.new_window )
        self.button1.grid( row = 0, column = 1, columnspan = 2,
sticky = W+E+N+S )
    def new_window(self):
        self.newWindow = karl2()
class karl2(Frame):
    def __init__(self):
        new =tk.Frame.__init__(self)
        new = Toplevel(self)
        new.title("karlos More Window")
        new.button = tk.Button( text = "PRESS TO CLOSE", width =
25,
```

```
        command = self.close_window )
    new.button.pack()
  def close_window(self):
    self.destroy()
def main():
  karl().mainloop()
if __name__ == '__main__':
  main()
```

As we go through with this, we are going to see that there are going to be a few standards that we are able to work with the GUI's and some of the attributes that go with it. Some of these are going to include options like bitmaps, anchors, cursors, colors, fonts, and dimensions.

What is CGI?

Until this point, a lot of the programming that we are able to do, whether it is with Python or another option, was not related that much to the network or for being online. But now it is time for us to move onto a bit of work with CGI. As the name suggests, CGI is going to mean the Common gateway interface for everything that we need to accomplish. CGI is going to be one of the more essential parts that we need to learn when it is time to work with HTTP.

To make it simple, this CGI is going to be a set of standards that is able to define the method that is considered standard when it is time to pass information or web-user requests to an application program, and then to get data back from it in order to pass that data on to the users you are working with. This is going to be an exchange of the information that happens between the web-server and a custom script.

When the user goes through this process and actually requests the web page that they want to work with, the server, when the process is working well, will send them that web page, rather than another one, that was requested. This is because the web server that you are working with is usually going to pass the information to all of the different programs of application that will process this data, and then it will make sure that an acknowledged message is going to show up. This may seem like a fairly basic process, but there are going to be a number of steps that happen with it. And the techniques that are used here, the ones that make sure that the data and the information are based back and forth between the application and the server will be CGI or Common Gateway Interface. It is as simple as that.

With this in mind, the first thing that we are going to take a look at is the first step of the process. Think about what happens when a user clicks on a hyperlink in order to browse on a particular URL or a web page that we have searched. To help us get started, there are a few steps that we are able to use, and these steps are going to include the following:

1. The browser is able to contact the web server of HTTP with a demand for the URL that is needed.
2. Then the URL is going to go through some parsing.
3. The system is going to look for the filename that was requested in the first step.
4. It is going to be able to find that file unless there is something wrong with the web page that was requested and will send it back.
5. The web browser is able to take these responses to form the webserver.
6. As the server response, it is either going to show you the file that it received, which is hopefully the website you asked for if all went well, or it is going to show us an error message.

Now, keep in mind with this one that it is possible to set up this HTTP server because when a certain directory is requested, then the file will not be sent back sometimes. Instead, it is going to be executed in this situation as a program, and then the output of that program is going to be the part that is displayed back to the browser you are using.

From here, we need to take a look at how we can configure the CGI that we want to work with. There are a number of steps that we are able to use to make this happen will include some of the following:

1. First, we want to be able to find out which user is running the web server at that time.

2. Then we will move on and check for the server configuration to help us figure out if we are then able to run in the scripts that are needed for that directory we are looking out.

3. Check out the permissions that are on that particular file.

4. Make a clear assurance that scripts you are making are readable and that the webserver user is going to be able to execute it as well.

5. Make sure that the scripts of Python have the first line set up in order to refer to the web server that the interpreter is able and willing to run.

And before we end with the discussion of CGI, we need to figure take a look at the structure of writing out one of these programs. The output of the script for CGI in Python is going to consist of two different sections, and they are going to be separated out thanks to a blank line. the first part is going to be there to show us the number of headers that we are meant to work with and that will be able to help us to describe back to our client what kind of data is following next. A good example of how this code is supposed to look and how we can structure out one of our CGI programs in Python will include the following:

print ("Content-Type : text/HTML")

```
# then comes the rest hyper-text documents
print ("<html>")
print ("<head>")
print ("<title>My First CGI-Program </title>")
print ("<head>")
print ("<body>")
print ("<h3>This is HTML's Body section </h3>")
print ("</body>")
print ("</html>")
```

Working with both the GUI and the CGI is going to be important with many of the projects that you are able to do within the Python coding language. When you are able to put all of these pieces together and see the great results, and you learn when you should pull each one up and use it, you will find that it is easier than ever to add in the amount of success that you would like to have in the process.

Conclusion

Thank you for making it through to the end of *Python Crash Course*. I hope it was informative and able to provide you with all of the tools you need to achieve your goals whatever they may be. The next step is to start using some of the different topics that we have discussed in this guidebook to your advantage and learn how to work with the Python language. There are a lot of different parts that can come with this kind of coding language, and learning how they all fit together and trying out some of the different codes that are present is one of the best ways to get hands-on and ready to go with this process.

This guide spent some time taking a look at some of the different tasks that you are able to do with the Python language, and how you are able to make this the right option for you as well. This book is meant to teach you all of the different parts that come with coding in general, but even more specifically what you are able to do with the help of this language whether you are starting as a total beginner or if you have been doing programming for a long period of time.

Working with coding is not always as easy as we would like, but you will find that when you take on the OOP language of Python, and you learn how to handle some of the basics, there is very little that you won't be able to do with your work. Trying out a few of these options and learning how to make it all fit together to write some fantastic codes.

There may be a lot of different options that you are going to work with when it is time to handle some of your biggest coding challenges. But the best one to choose is going to be Python. It has all of the strength that you are looking for, a lot of ease to learn and to read, and so much more. When you are ready to get your crash course in the Python language and you are ready to hit the ground running, make sure to check out this guidebook to get started.